Medusa and Her Curse

Children's Greek & Roman Myths

BABY PROFESSOR

EDUCATION KIDS

Let's learn some interesting
facts about Medusa, a monster
in Greek mythology.

What do you know
about Medusa?
What comes to your
mind when you
hear this name?

**Read on and find
out about this
powerful creature
and her curse.**

Meet the hideous
creature…

Medusa was
exceedingly ugly.
She had a lot of
poisonous snakes
on her head instead
of hair. In other
words, Medusa
was a monster.

She was one of the Gorgon sisters, along with Sthenno and Euryale. Of them, Medusa was the only mortal. Medusa's parents were Phorcys and Ceto. Her grandparents were Gaea (Earth) and Oceanus.

The Once Beautiful Medusa…

In the myth, Medusa was originally a very beautiful maiden. She was golden-haired. Her dazzling beauty attracted Poseidon, the god of the sea. She was once a priestess of Athena. She vowed to stay single and not to get married.

However, she fell in love with Poseidon, and married him. She totally forgot what she had promised. Because of this, Medusa was terribly punished. The Goddess Athena transformed her into a scaly gorgon. What happened to her was beyond her control.

Athena was a
powerful goddess.
Medusa's hair
became venomous
snakes. Her loving
and beautiful eyes
became red. Medusa
turned into a very
ugly monster!

The Ugly Monster...

When Medusa
saw her ugly
transformation as a
disgusting creature,
she ran away and
never returned to
her home. She was
rejected and shunned
by the whole world.

According to the
myth, Medusa fled
to Africa. She was
hopeless and she
became as bad in her
actions as she was
bad to look at. As she
wandered in Africa,
baby snakes fell from
her head—the myth
is trying to explain
why there were a lot
of snakes in Africa.

Medusa's hideous appearance reflected her character. The once kind and beautiful Medusa was transformed into a disgusting, wicked creature.

The Curse...

BENVENVTVS CELLINVS

Medusa was cursed by Athena. Whoever would stare at her would turn into stone. This was Medusa's curse. Medusa was killed by Perseus, one of the amazing Greek heroes who was sent by Athena.

He killed Medusa
and let her turn into
stone herself, in this
way: he put a mirror
in front of Medusa
that made her see
her own reflection.

After she became a stone, Perseus cut off Medusa's head and made it into a weapon. He defeated all his enemies by using Medusa's head, since anyone who saw it turned into stone. As the Greek hero cut off Medusa's head, the winged horse, Pegasus and the hero of the Golden sword, Chrysaor, sprang from Medusa's body.

Perseus gave
Medusa's head to
the goddess Athena
to be placed on her
shield. Athena used
Medusa's scaly
skin to make an
impenetrable shield.

Visit
BABY PROFESSOR
EDUCATION KIDS
www.BabyProfessorBooks.com
to download Free Baby Professor eBooks
and view our catalog of new and exciting
Children's Books